Gold Stars®

Starting to Write

Pre-school

Written by Betty Root

PaRragon

Bath · New York · Singapore · Hong Kong · Cologne · Delhi · Melbourne

Gold Stars®

Helping your child

⭐ Remember that the activities in this book should be enjoyed by your child. Try to find a quiet place to work.

⭐ Your child does not need to complete each page in one go. **Always stop before your child grows tired**, and come back to the same page another time.

⭐ It is important to work through the pages in the right order because the activities do get progressively more difficult.

⭐ The answers to the activities are on page 32.

⭐ Always give your child lots of encouragement and praise.

⭐ Remember that the gold stars and badges are a reward for effort as well as for achievement.

Illustrated by Simon Abbott

This edition published by Parragon in 2010

Parragon
Queen Street House
4 Queen Street
BATH, BA1 1HE, UK

ISBN 978-1-4075-7530-8
Printed in China

Contents

Making patterns

Trace over the dotted lines. Make a row underneath.

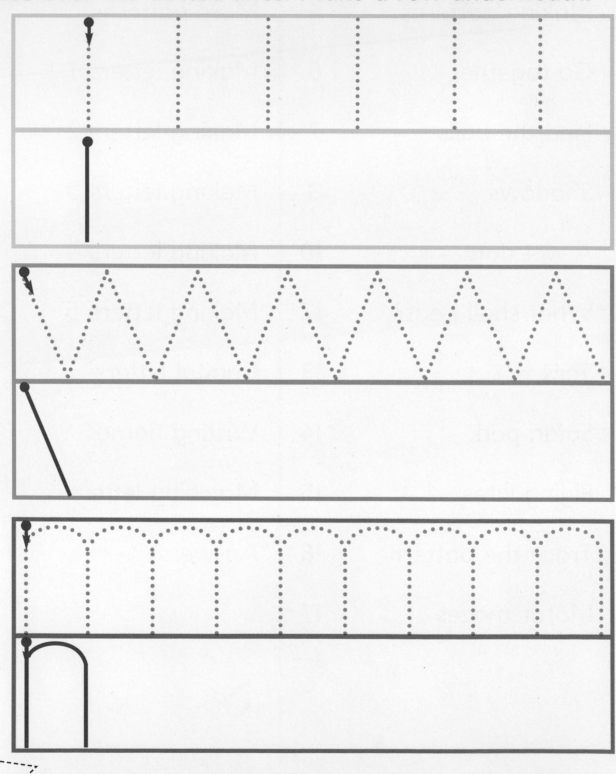

Note for parent: This activity gives practice in pencil control in preparation for letter shapes.

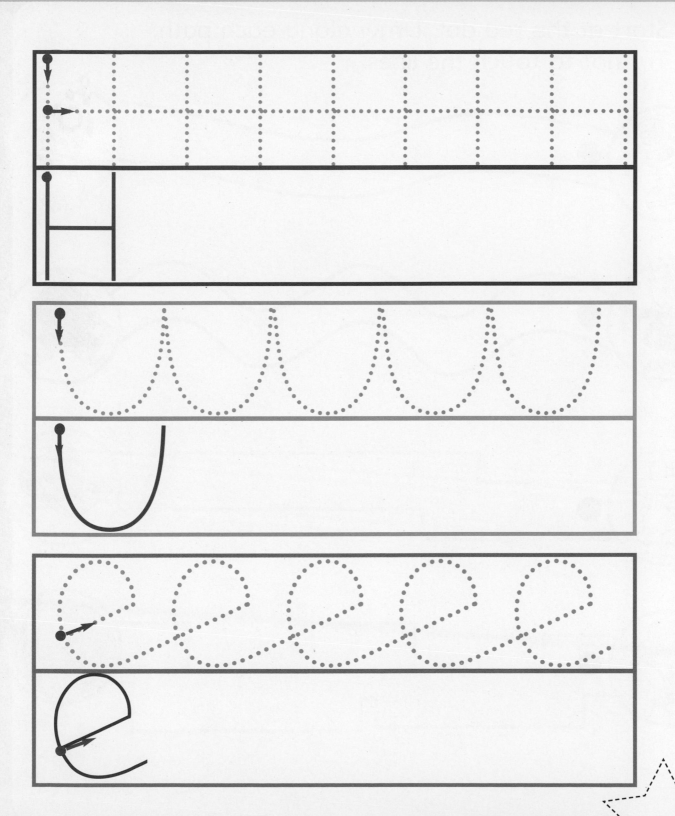

Go together

Start at the red dot. Draw along each path.
Try not to touch the lines.

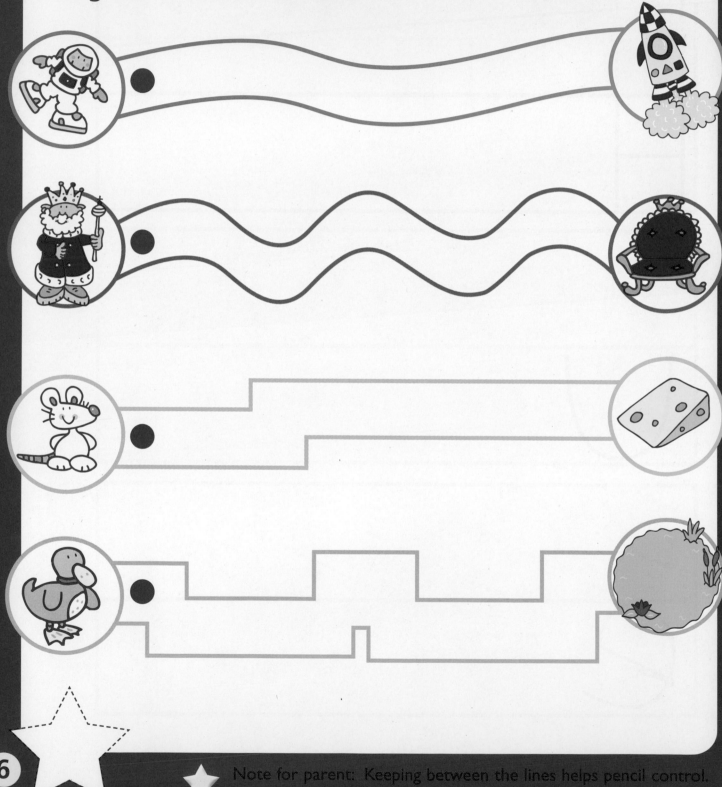

Note for parent: Keeping between the lines helps pencil control.

Find the balls

Find 5 balls in the picture.
Draw a circle around each one.
Finish the pattern of circles around the picture.
Colour the picture.

Shadows

Draw lines to join each picture to its shadow.
Try to make straight lines.
The first one has been done for you.

Draw lines to join each picture to its shadow.
Try to make wiggly lines.
The first one has been done for you.

A wet day

Draw over the dotted lines to finish the picture.
Colour the picture.

10

Note for parent: This activity helps children to use a pencil carefully to complete pictures.

What shall I eat?

Start at the red dot. Draw along each path to find out what everyone eats.

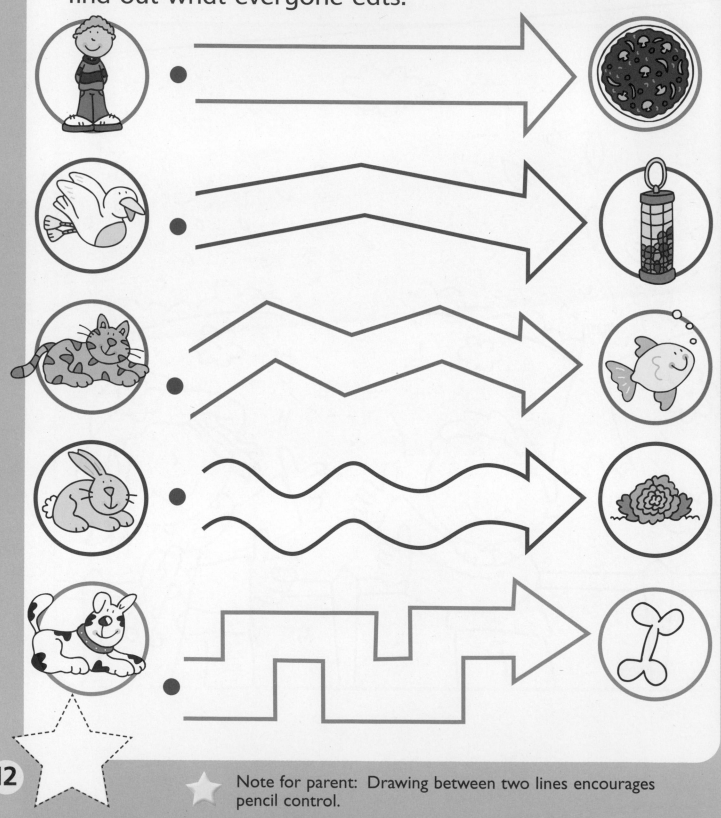

Note for parent: Drawing between two lines encourages pencil control.

Tails

Draw over the dotted lines.
Colour the animals.

 Note for parent: Children need to develop a steady hand for good writing.

13

Safari park

Draw over the dotted lines.
Colour the picture.

14

Note for parent: This activity helps children to use a pencil carefully to complete pictures.

Flying kites

Draw over the dotted lines.
Colour the kites to match the T-shirts.

Note for parent: This gives children practice in controlling the direction of their pencil.

15

Trace the pattern

Trace over the dotted lines on each ball.

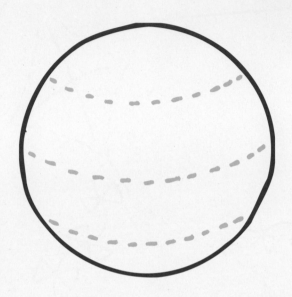

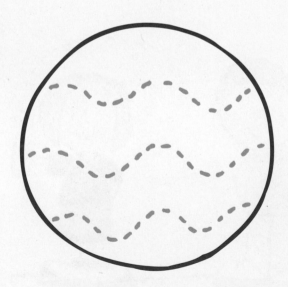

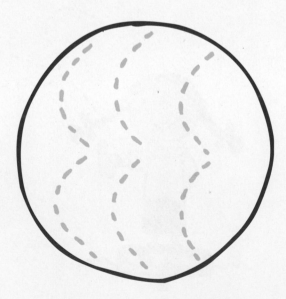

 Note for parent: This activity gives children further practice in pencil control.

Motor mazes

Trace over the dotted lines to find out which car will get to the flag first.

Note for parent: This gives children practice in controlling the direction of their pencil.

17

More patterns

Trace over the lines to finish the pictures.

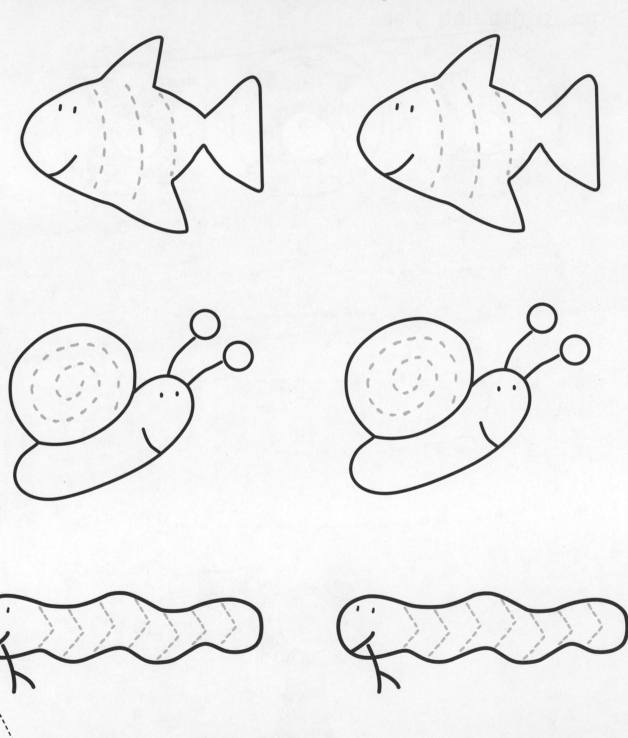

Note for parent: This activity helps children to follow dotted lines to make a pattern.

Making letters 1

Trace over each dotted letter.

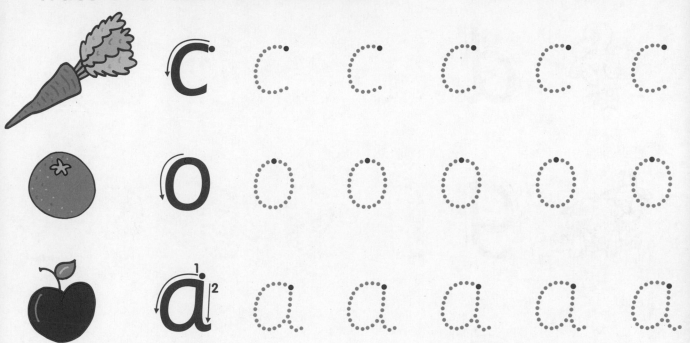

c c c c c c

o o o o o o

a a a a a a

Trace the letters to complete the words.

orange

apple

carrot

Note for parent: This activity helps children to write the letters c, o and a.

Making letters 2

Trace over each dotted letter.

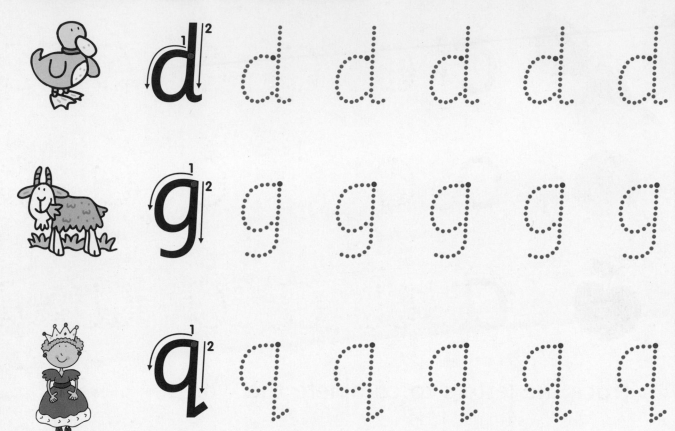

d d d d d d

g g g g g g

q q q q q q

Circle the picture which begins with the letter d.

 Note for parent: This activity helps children to write the letters d, g, q, b, h and p.

Trace over each dotted letter.

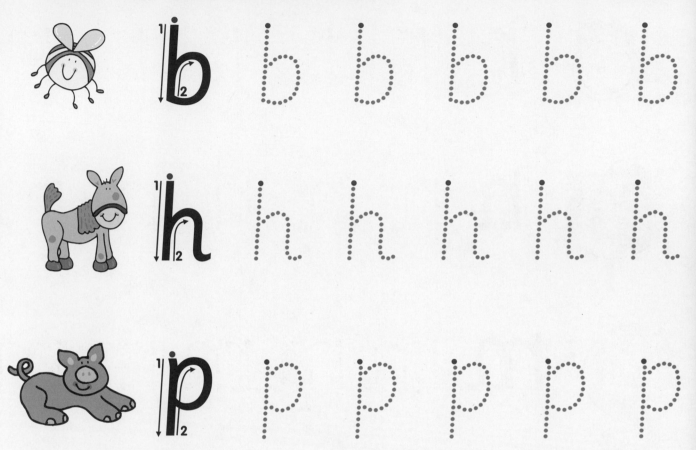

b b b b b b

h h h h h h

p p p p p p

Say the name of each picture and write its beginning letter.

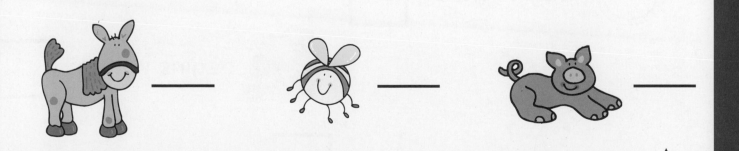

Making letters 3

Trace over each dotted letter.

Put a tick or a cross in each box. Yes ✓ No ✗

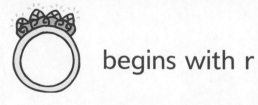 begins with r ☐

 begins with m ☐

 begins with n ☐

22

Note for parent: This activity helps children to write the letters r, n, m, u and y.

Trace over each dotted letter.

Trace the letters to complete the words.

sun

umbrella

yellow

yo-yo

23

Making letters 4

Trace over the dotted letters.

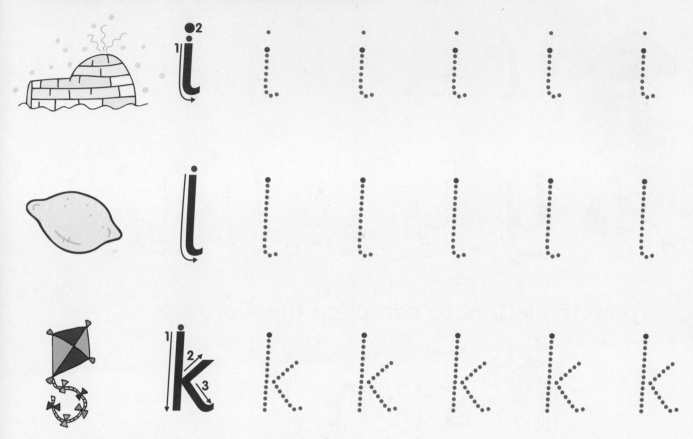

i i i i i i

l l l l l l

k k k k k k

Circle the picture which begins with the letter k.

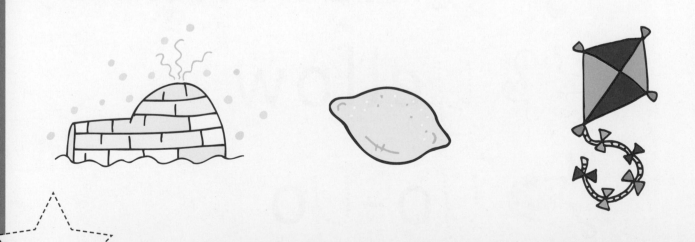

24

Note for parent: This activity helps children write the letters i, l, k, f, j and t.

Trace over the dotted letters.

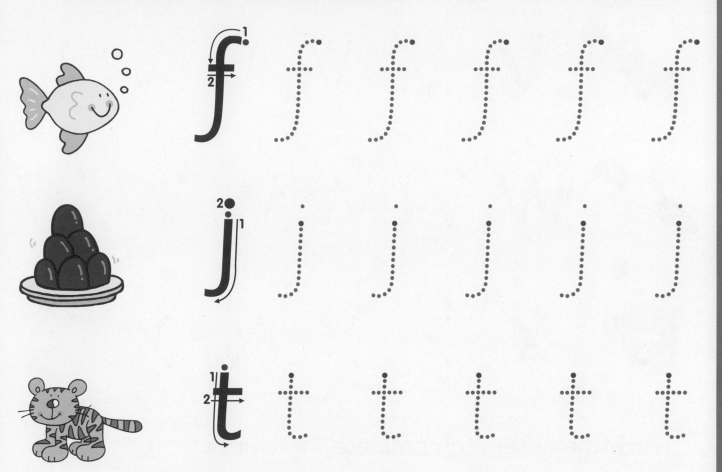

Say the name of each picture.
Cross out the letter which is wrong.

f
t

j
f

Making letters 5

Trace over the dotted letters.

v v v v v v v

w w w w w w w

x x x x x x

Trace the letters to complete the words.

 violin

 x-ray

 watch

Note for parent: This activity helps children to write the letters v, w, x, z, e and s.

Trace over the dotted letters.

Z z z z z z

e e e e e e

s s s s s s

Draw lines to join the pictures that start in the same way.

Capital letters

Capital letters are used at the beginning of names and other important words.
Trace over the dotted lines to make the letters.

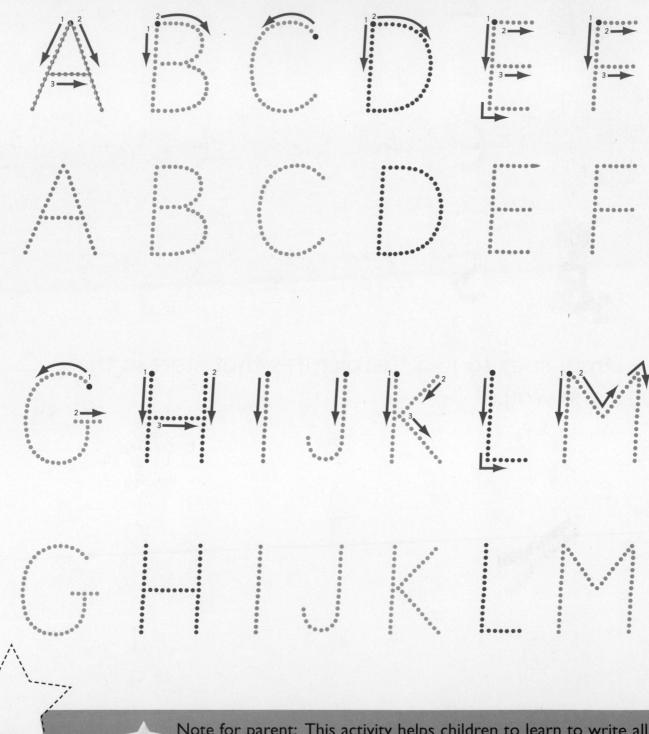

 Note for parent: This activity helps children to learn to write all the capital letters.

N O P Q R S T

N O P Q R S T

U V W X Y Z

U V W X Y Z

Writing names

All names begin with a capital letter.
Write the names and colour the pictures.
Draw a picture of yourself and write your name.

Mummy

Daddy

Granny

30

Note for parent: This activity helps children to learn that names begin with a capital letter.

Matching letters

Trace over the dotted letters. Draw lines to join each letter to a picture that begins with the same letter.

a h b k f n

m p u z r l

Note for parent: This activity gives practice in writing and matching letters.

31

Answers

Page 7

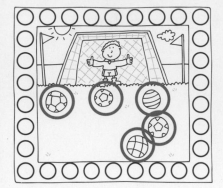

Pages 8–9

Page 15

Page 17

Page 20
Duck begins with the letter d.

Page 21
horse, bee, pig.

Page 22

 begins with r. ☑

 begins with n. ☒

 begins with m. ☒

Page 24
Kite begins with the letter k.

Page 25

 | f ⟋
 | j ⟋

Page 27

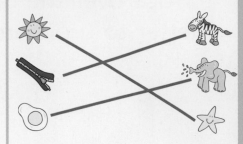

Page 31

32